THE BOOK
of
DORMIN'

THE BOOK
of
DORMIN'

*A Sacredly Cheeky Guide to Starting
Life in College*

By Shane & Casie Stephens

Edited By Blair Parke

HOLIDORM
DECK YOUR DORM

holidorm.com | @holidorm_

Published in the United States by Holidorm Austin, TX

ISBN: 979-8-9995630-0-2

Library of Congress Control Number: 2025915120

FIRST EDITION

Book Design: Holidorm.com

Editor: Blair Parke

Presented To:

_____

_____

Date:

_____

This book is dedicated to:
Bug, Bub, & Baby Kate

Perhaps you found this book left in a dorm room drawer or perhaps your aunt bought it for you at graduation. However you came upon it, we're glad that you have it. Share it with others as you see fit...

The Main Canon

Table of Contents

Introduction to The Book of Dormin'

College is one of the most exciting, overwhelming, and transformative seasons in one's life. It's where laundry piles high, sleep runs low, and caffeine becomes a love language. But it's also where identity is formed, friendships are forged, and purpose begins to take shape.

Inspired by conversations with our own college-bound kids, *The Book of Dormin'* was created to help students make that leap—from home to dorm, from dependence to adulthood—with a bit of wit, a touch of wisdom, and lot of love.

Written in a style that blends comical ancient verse with modern college reality, this book offers practical lessons for everyday life: how to wash your clothes, clean your bathroom, make your bed (like you actually mean it), manage money, resolve conflict, and even stay out of jail. Read it as you will, pick it up, put it down, binge it like your favorite Netflix series, or just store it near your favorite reading throne.

It is much more than just a survival guide. We've included an Apocrypha (big word ... we know) with eternal truths we've learned the hard way—about responsibility, relationships, purpose, and faith. These are the kinds of lessons that don't always show up in a class syllabus but matter just as much as anything you'll learn in a lecture hall.

We hope *The Book of Dormin'* gives you tools to thrive in this new season—and also gives you space to reflect, grow, and ask the bigger questions about life, faith, and who you're becoming. But most of all, we hope it makes you smile—not just because of the odd way it is written, but because you'll learn that you have a God who loves you.

So, laugh a little. Learn a lot. And remember that Jesus is found not just in Sunday school classes—He loves dorm rooms too.

Love, Shane and Casie

Prologue

A Preface Unto the Youth Who Dwelleth in Tiny Quarters

1 Behold, this is the record of the generations of those who went forth from the house of their fathers and mothers, entering into the land of College.

2 Yea, they departed from the place of comfort, where laundry was done without request, and food didst appear as manna upon the table.

3 And they dwelt in dorm rooms and apartments not larger than a prophet's tent, sharing their space with strangers and brethren alike,

4 And verily, they knew not how to fold a fitted sheet, nor how long a burrito should be microwaved without peril.

5 But the spirit of learning was upon them, and they sought after knowledge—not only from books and tests, but also that of wisdom which leadeth unto life:

6 The art of adulting, the discipline of the dish rag, and the gospel of the shared fridge.

7 Wherefore, this book hath been prepared—a guide, a light, and a balm to the inexperienced soul—

8 That whosoever shall read it and apply its teachings with diligence and humor shall not perish under piles of laundry, nor be cast out by roommates in wrath.

9 For behold, each chapter containeth instruction in the ways of independent living, written with gladness and cheek, that it might not be grievous unto thee,

10 But rather a joy and a help, even a shield, against the slings of unwashed dishes and the arrows of financial struggle.

11 Therefore, receive ye this book with thanksgiving, and let not thy pride keep thee from the learning of such simple things.

12 For the wise person cleaneth their toilet, while the foolish one waiteth until guests are at the door.

13 Let the youth who would dwell in peace and pass their courses study these words,

14 And let the children of wisdom write them upon sticky notes and bathroom mirrors.

15 For this is the Book of Dormin'—a manual of mirth and might—for all who go forth to dwell on their own for the first time, away from parental figures.

16 Let the reader laugh, and let the listener hearken. Let socks be sorted and ramen be rationed.

17 And may grace and Febreze be multiplied unto thee, from orientation until graduation.

18 Go team. Amen.

Chapter 1: The Book of Washings

Concerning the Cleansing of Garments

Chapter 1: The Book of Washings

Concerning the Cleansing of Garments

1 Hearken, O youth, and incline thine ear unto wisdom; for the day shall come when thy garments shall be many and stained with the doings of life.

2 Therefore, prepare thyself. Learn the order of washing, lest thy raiment be spoiled and thy shame be great among thy roommates.

3 First, thou shalt gather thy clothes from off the floor and from the corners of thy dwelling, yea, even from under the bed and behind the chair.

4 Separate thy garments by their kind: the whites with the whites, the darks with the darks, and the colors that are bright with others like unto them.

5 Wash not the red garment unto the white, lest it bleed and cause mourning.

6 And examine each piece, whether it be delicate or strong; for the delicate requireth gentler cycles and the strong shall endure greater trials.

7 Take thou a soap of washing—be it liquid or powdered—and pour it according to the measure written by the manufacturer, not more or less.

8 For verily, too much soap bringeth forth froth and ruin, and the residue shall cleave unto thy clothes as a curse and too less would make thy clothing unclean.

9 Place the garments in the machine, not exceeding its bounds, for the washer is not without limits.

10 Choose wisely the settings thereon: cold for the colored, warm for the sturdy, and gentle for those things thou lovest most.

11 When the washing is accomplished, remove thy garments speedily, lest they become damp like tombs and stinketh.

12 Cast them into the dryer with a faithful heart or hang them around the room with clothespins made fast.

13 Remove them when they are dry from the dryer and fold them with diligence, that they be not wrinkled nor lost.

14 And lo, if thy garments are clean but crumpled, resembling the linen of the neglected.

15 Take thou the iron, hot and hissing like the breath of discipline, and lay it gently upon thy fabric.

16 Smooth the front as thou would thy face before a date, and the collar as a priest prepares his robe before the holy day.

17 Let not the iron linger in one place, lest thou scorch thy garments and enter the fellowship of the burned.

18 He who forgetteth to use water in his iron shall wrestle forever with wrinkles and be known as one of the Disciples of Disarray.

19 Remember this commandment: *Thou shalt check the tag, for not all fabrics receive the heat of the iron without protest.*

20 Follow these teachings, and thus shalt be clean; and thy garments shall be made perfect and soft—a joy unto thee, and a wonder unto thy neighbors.

21 For cleanliness is next to godliness, and order bringeth peace to the soul. Amen.

Chapter 2: The Book of Order

Concerning the Cleansing of the Bathroom and the Tidying of Habitations

Chapter 2: The Book of Order

Concerning the Cleansing of the Bathroom and the Tidying of Habitations

1 Thus saith wisdom: Let not filth abide in thy dwelling, neither let uncleanness have dominion over the place where thou liest down and risest up, as well as where guests visitith.

2 For they who abideth in squalor shall surely reap chaos, and they who neglecteth the toilet shall be forsaken by roommates.

3 Therefore, on the first day of the week—or on the day that seemeth good unto thee—set thine hand to the work, procrastinating not.

4 Begin thou in the bathroom, where many unclean evils lurk unseen.

5 Take up the brush of scrubbing and cleanse the bowl of the toilet with fervor, using cleanser that foameth and vanquisheth the hidden grime.

6 Flush thou the waters afterward; be not afraid, for the swirl thereof is mighty and shall carry away that which is unclean.

7 Wipe down the sink and remove the toothpaste that hardeneth like unto mortar from past over squishes of the tube.

8 Yea, even the mirror shall thou cleanse that thy reflection may not be marred by the spittle of thy brushing.

9 Take also a sanitized cloth, or paper of absorbent nature, and apply it unto the counter, the faucet, and the handles of the door, which are touched by many hands, clean and unclean.

10 Spray thou the tub with the holy mixture of soap and vinegar, or a cleaner sold among the nations, and scrub with great zeal until it shineth as glass.

11 Empty the bin of trash, for the refuse doth stink if it tarrieth too long and becometh an abomination unto the nostrils.

12 Lay out fresh towels and hang them properly, that the place may be pleasant and orderly before thy guests arrive.

13 Now concerning thy personal living space—make thy bed each morning, as a soldier preparing for the day of battle.

14 For lo, a made bed setteth the tone for righteousness and bringeth peace to the soul.

15 Dust thou the shelves and the top of the fridge, sweeping or vacuuming the floor weekly that crumbs and hairballs multiply not like the locusts of Egypt.

16 If thy dwelling art blessed with a kitchenette, let no dish remain in the sink past the setting of the sun, lest evil odors and mildew rise up and judgment fall upon thee.

17 Keep things in their place, for every item hath a home, and confusion cometh when nothing is where it belongeth.

18 Store thy shoes by the door, thy snacks in containers, and thy chargers not upon thine enemies' desk.

19 And if thou sharest the space with others, be thou considerate and quick to clean what thou hast soiled personally.

20 For blessed is the roommate who cleaneth after themselves, and woe unto they who leaveth their hair in the drain.

21 Keep these statutes so peace shall dwell within thy halls, and thy dwelling shall be a haven, yea, even a sanctuary, amidst the trials of college life.

22 Let it be written. Let it be wiped. Amen.

Chapter 3: The Book of The Bed

Concerning the Order of the Bed and the Casting Out of Crumbs

Chapter 3: The Book of The Bed

Concerning the Order of the Bed and the Casting Out of Crumbs

1 And it came to pass on the first morn of independent living that the student rose from slumber and beheld their bed they were in, and lo—it was a pit of disorder.

2 The sheets were twisted like the cords of confusion, the blanket lay half upon the floor, and the pillow had fled unto the far corner of the room.

3 And the student said, within their heart, "Doth it truly matter? For who shall see this mess, save I?"

4 But a whisper came unto them—yea, the Spirit of Discipline—and it saith, *"They who maketh their bed shall also maketh progress in their day."*

5 Therefore, take heed: Rise thou up and stretch forth thy hand, straightening the sheet with diligence.

6 Pull ye the corners tight, like unto the skin of a drum, that it wrinkle not beneath thee nor bunch up like a serpent in the night.

7 Lay thy blanket with evenness upon the frame and smootheth it, from end to end, with the palm of thy hand.

8 Fluff thy pillow and smite it gently that it regain its countenance and comfort thy weary head in the hour of rest.

9 Fold thou the edge of the top sheet and blanket with care, so it may appear pleasing to the eye and not as chaos incarnate.

10 Tuck not as unto a mummy, lest thy feet rise in rebellion; neither leave it flapping to and fro, like a banner of apathy.

11 Let this bed be a temple of rest, not a nest of tangled sorrow.

12 For thou art worthy of a bed well made, and thy future spouse shall bless thy name for learning this in thy youth.

13 And if thine eyes be tempted to delay, saying, *"I shall return to bed soon anyway,"* remember this:
"They who maketh their bed ruleth over sloth,
And they who maketh it not shall reap the whirlwind of crumbs and regret."

14 Moreover, take not thy meals upon the bed, for such things defile the sacred linens.

15 And they who sleepeth in the garments of their daily routine hath already lost the battle.

16 Wash thy sheets every seventh day, or thereabouts, for though thou seest no filth, lo, it aboundeth still.

17 And they who lieth in unwashed bedding shall be known by their smell and remembered not fondly by others.

18 So let order reign, even in thine unseen chambers. For they who conquereth the bed conquers also the day.

19 Let this be a sign unto thy future self that thou wert once young and yet wise.

20 And it shall be known through all the land: *Behold, here sleepeth one who hath their life somewhat together.* Amen.

Chapter 4: The Book of Fix

**Concerning the Care and Upkeep of Thy Dwelling,
That It Become Not a Pit of Sorrows**

Chapter 4: The Book of Fix

Concerning the Care and Upkeep of Thy Dwelling, That It Become Not a Pit of Sorrows

1 And it came to pass that the student returned to his dorm and flipped the switch, and behold—there was no light.

2 And they cried out in despair, saying, *"Surely this is the end!"*

3 But lo, the lightbulb had perished, not the power, and the solution was simple—yet unknown to them.

4 Therefore, hear now the words of the wise: If thou wilt dwell in a place, thou must learn to maintain it with thine own hands, lest mildew and dorm maintenance requests consume thee.

5 If thy light flickereth or goeth out altogether, be not afraid. First, turn off the switch and let the bulb cool, lest thy fingers be scorched.

6 Twist thou bulb gently, counterclockwise, to remove and replace it with one of the same kind and wattage. Touch not the metal, lest the shock of thine impatience travel through thee like lightning through the rod.

7 Rejoice, for light hath returned to thy study corner, and darkness shall not reign over thy laundry pile.

8 If thou livest in a place with an air system, the filter thereof must be changed every month or two, lest dust become thy portion and allergies thy affliction.

9 Remove the old with care and insert the new, according to its measures and arrows, so thy lungs may rejoice and thy air be not musty.

10 If water pool beneath thy feet whilst showering, and the drain doth not gurgle with joy, then surely it is clogged.

11 Fear not, for thou shalt use the mighty staff called the plunger. Place it firmly over the drain and press with vigor, as if rebuking a demon.

12 Should hair be the culprit of the clogged drain, retrieve it with a wire hook or thy trembling hand. Let not pride keep thee from the nasty deed—for cleanliness requireth great courage.

13 Pour thou hot water, or a mixture of baking soda and vinegar, that the pipes may be cleansed without wrath.

14 If thy toilet overfloweth or refuseth to flush, be swift and strong. Reach for the plunger—yea, that trusty staff of salvation.

15 Ensure it sealeth over the hole and push down with faith and rhythm. If it resisteth still, call upon maintenance, and do not pretend it was thy roommate's fault. The maintenance crew careth not.

16 Remember, flush not what ought not to be flushed: wipes that lie and say they art "flushable," thy roommate's sadness, nor toothpicks, nor ramen.

17 Knowest thou when to fix and when to call for help. If sparks fly, mold doth multiply, or the heat leaveth entirely, submit a maintenance request with haste and detail.

18 Be not passive nor delayeth the email, lest thou be without light, warmth, or water for days.

19 And lo, keepeth a kit for thy own use: lightbulbs, gloves, plunger, screwdriver, duct tape, and air freshener. All is the incense of dorm sanctification.

20 Blessed is the one who knoweth how to unclog, replace, scrub, and seal.

21 For they shall dwell in peace and not in stench, and their roommates shall call them heroes of the hall.

22 And the RA shall nod with respect, and maintenance shall reply quickly, saying, *"At last, one who knoweth what they're doing."*

23 Let order be in thy bathroom, light in thy ceiling, and filters in thy vents, that thy dwelling may be a place of comfort and not chaos.

24 Amen, and flush with honor.

Chapter 5: The Book of Coin

Concerning Thy Card Be Not Declined in the Hour of Need

Chapter 5: The Book of Coin

Concerning Thy Card Be Not Declined in thy Hour of Need

1 Hearken, O ye that spend, and incline thine heart unto prudence: for the wallet is not bottomless, and the debit card fainteth when thou swipe it without thought.

2 For many are the temptations of the campus: overpriced coffee, food delivered by chariots on wheels, and subscriptions thou forgettest to cancel.

3 Yea, even the vending machine calleth unto thee in the hour of weakness, saying, *"Just one more candy bar—ye shall not surely overdraft."*

4 Therefore, write down thy increase—whether it be from parents, part-time labors, or scholarships of mercy.

5 And make thou a budget with thine increase, which is a holy plan of spending that thou mayest know where thy treasure goeth, not being surprised when it is no more.

6 Divide thy shekels into portions. One part for housing and bills that thou mayest not be cast into the street. Another part for groceries and nourishment, so thy belly be not empty; and a portion for savings, that thou mayest not panic when thy tire bursteth or thy laptop descendeth into darkness. Leave also a small portion for joy and for giving, for life is more than instant noodles and regret.

7 Track thy spending, yea even with an app upon thy phone or with pencil and notebook, if thou art of the old school.

8 Be thou honest and write down the $7 iced coffee, even when it stingeth. For truth bringeth awareness, and awareness is the beginning of wisdom.

9 Touch not the credit card without understanding, for though it smileth upon thee in the moment, in the end, it biteth like unto a serpent with interest.

10 And if thou usest credit, pay it swiftly and in full, lest the debt rise up like a storm and drown thee.

11 Be not deceived by sales, for every "50% off" is still a full price if thou needest it not.

12 Ask thyself always, "Is this a need, or merely a shiny thing that delighteth my eyes for a season?"

13 Learn to cook, and thou shalt save; brew thy own coffee, and thou shalt prosper; walk when thou canst, and verily, thou shalt be blessed in wallet and thigh.

14 Beware the spirit of "treat thyself," for though it speaketh sweetly, it emptieth thy accounts with stealth, leaving behind only crumbs.

15 Rejoice when thou findest free food on campus, and marketh well the times and locations of such sacred gatherings.

16 For blessed is the student who feasteth on free pizza, for their budget shall endure.

17 Let contentment dwell in thy heart, and not comparison with thy neighbor who driveth a shiny car and weareth many brand names.

18 For thou knowest not their balance, neither the depth of their debt.

19 And if thou stumble in thy spending, rise up and try again. For mercy is great, and overdraft fees, though terrible, are not the end.

20 In budgeting, there is freedom, and in planning, there is peace.

21 Ye that is faithful with little shall one day be master over much—and maybe own furniture not found upon the curb.

22 Thus endeth the chapter of wise spending. Go forth and may thy Venmo balance never fall into the red. Amen.

Chapter 6: The Book of Boo-Boos

Concerning the Ministering unto Fleshly Affliction and the Use of the Sacred Bandage

Chapter 6: The Book of Boo-Boos

Concerning the Ministering unto Fleshly Affliction and the Use of the Sacred Bandage

1 And it came to pass that the young person did grievously slice their thumb while preparing a sandwich, for they knew not the treachery of the serrated blade.

2 And they bled upon the cutting board, crying out unto their roommate, saying, *"Lo, I am undone!"*

3 But their roommate was wise, having been raised by a nurse of renown, and they did fetch the box of bandages and the sacred bottle of hydrogen peroxide.

4 And the roommate said, *"Fear not, for I shall teach thee the ways of minor wound care, that thou perish not of a minor cut."*

5 Thus, let it be known: When thou art cut, wash thy wound with soap and water, and blot it gently with a clean cloth.

6 Apply thou an antiseptic, so that bacteria may flee before thee, and cover it with a bandage as a cloak unto the afflicted flesh.

7 If the bleeding ceaseth not after many minutes, or if the wound gape like unto the mouth of a fish, seek medical aid, for thou mayest require stitches, and no, duct tape shall not suffice.

8 And if thou burn thy hand upon the stove cooking nuggies, or thy curling iron, or the deceitful microwave popcorn bag, place it under cool water without delay.

9 Hurt it not further with ice, which bringeth more harm than help, but soothe it gently and cover with a sterile dressing.

10 Should a fever rise within thee, know that thy body fighteth valiantly against unseen invaders.

11 Rest thou, hydrate greatly, and taketh acetaminophen or ibuprofen, according to the dosage inscribed upon the bottle.

12 Do not double the dose, neither mix medicines like a fool who readeth not the label.

13 Let every young adult have a box of healing provisions:
Bandages of many sizes
The balm of antibiotic ointment
Thermometer of truth
Pain relievers, both feverish and crampish,
And lo, antihistamines for the wrath of springtime.

14 And if thou awaken with affliction not known—such as swelling unnatural, rashes mysterious, or pain that shouteth in the night—call thou upon the nurse line or health center, where wisdom may guide thee.

15 For urgent care is for the moderately serious, and emergency rooms are for the truly dire.

16 Go not unto the ER for a hangnail, lest thou be smitten with great copays and eye-rolls from the nurses.

17 Google not thy symptoms in the midnight hour, for that path leadeth only unto madness and declarations of doom.

18 Thy sniffles are not the plague, and thy headache is not surely a tumor.

19 Ask for help when thou art unsure, and ignore not that still, small voice within that sayeth, "Maybe thou should not ignore that lump."

20 For it is not a weakness to seek professional care, but wisdom. And those who go early are often healed quickly, while those who delay shall end up calling their mother in tears.

21 So let it be written in the Book of Dormin': Keep thou thy medicine box stocked, thy wounds clean, and thy pride low enough to ask for help.

22 And may health follow thee like a shadow that walketh in the sun. Amen.

Chapter 7: The Book of Responsibility

Concerning the Daily March and the Stewardship of Time

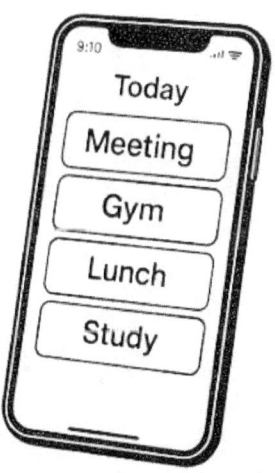

Chapter 7: The Book of Responsibility

Concerning the Daily March and the Stewardship of Time

1 And it came to pass in the days of syllabi and surprise quizzes that the student did forget the due date of a paper, and much weeping and gnashing of teeth ensued.

2 For though the professor spoke of the paper plainly, and it was written in bold upon the course page, yet the student had not written it down, nor set a reminder, nor pondered the flow of their days at school.

3 And so the student cried, *"Why is my life chaos?"*

4 But a still, small voice answered, saying, *"Because thou treatest thy brain as a filing cabinet, not as a garden to be tended."*

5 Therefore, hear now the commandment: *Write thou things down, and ye shall be free.*

6 Take unto thyself a planner, be it of paper, or digital scroll, or calendar synced with the cloud.

7 Mark thereon thy classes, thy work shifts, thy due dates, and thy appointments, both sacred and ridiculous.

8 Review thy planner at the dawn of each day, like a warrior surveying the battlefield.

9 And plan not only for the great tasks, but also for the small: the brushing of teeth, the replying of emails, the calling of thy mother.

10 Let not thy day rule over thee like a cruel master, but break it into pieces, assigning each task a time and a place.

11 For the idle hour devoureth the focused mind, and lo, TikTok shall consume the better part of thy week if thou art not vigilant.

12 Say not, "I work better under pressure," for this is the lie of the sluggard and the anthem of the procrastinator.

13 For it is written: *They who prepareth early shall not pull the dreaded all-nighter, neither shall their printer smite him at 11:59.*

14 Build thee habits—morning rituals, afternoon routines, evening closures—that thy life may have rhythm and not flail like a furry rodent in traffic.

15 And know this: Multitasking is but a fable. For no man can scroll, study, snack, and succeed all at once.

16 Be thou realistic in thy scheduling, for thou art not a machine but a creature of flesh, caffeine, and distraction.

17 Schedule rest, that thou faint not; and margin, that thou overflow not; and snacks, that thou snap not.

18 And if thou forgettest a task, or falleth behind, despair not. For each sunrise is a divine "reset button," and mercy endureth until midterms.

19 For they who mastereth the calendar shall master their mind, and they who keepeth a to-do list shall not forget the milk nor the FAFSA.

20 Let thy yes be yes, and thy no be no. Overcommit not thyself, lest thou drown in a sea of obligations and group projects.

21 So go forth, O student, and make peace with the ticking of the clock. For time is not thy enemy, but thy inheritance.

22 And it shall be known in all the campus: *Behold, this one arriveth on time, remembereth their deadlines, and doth not cry over spilled Google Docs.*

23 Amen—and set a reminder.

Chapter 8: The Book of Knowing Thy Stuff

Concerning the Noble Pursuit of Wisdom and
Becoming More Knowledgeable Than Thy Parents

Chapter 8: The Book of Knowing
Thy Stuff

Concerning the Noble Pursuit of Wisdom and Becoming More Knowledgeable Than Thy Parents

1 And it came to pass that the student looked upon the mountain of syllabi and assignments, and knew not whether to cry or nap.

2 For they had come into the land of college, yet they knew not the purpose of their pilgrimage.

3 And so they cried, *"Why am I here? Is it not enough to pass the class and binge the shows of my people?"*

4 But lo, the voice of truth spoke unto them, saying, *"Thou art here to learn—to grow in wisdom, to sharpen thy mind, and to prepare thyself for life beyond the microwave."*

5 Therefore, gird up thy brain, O learner, and charge into thy classes with courage and clarity, and fear not the group project, though it be a den of slackers.

6 Attend thy lectures, even when the bed calleth out unto thee with sweet whispers and heated blankets.

7 For they who attendeth not class shall awaken one day to midterms and weepeth greatly.

8 Take thou good notes—not of everything but of that which actually mattereth.

9 Listen with both ears, highlight not thy entire article like a fool, and ask questions, for curiosity is the tinder of knowledge.

10 Study not as the sluggard who crammeth in the midnight hour, but as the wise steward who layeth aside time each day—and needeth not five energy drinks.

11 For repetition planteth the seed, and review watereth it, and lo—the harvest is understanding.

12 And when thou writest papers, cheat not, neither lifteth paragraphs from the Internet as if they were thine own.

13 For behold, the eye of Turnitin seeth all, and plagiarism is a snare that bringeth swift destruction of academic career.

14 Do thine own work, even when it is hard; for it is thy struggle that sharpeneth the mind, and effort is more honorable than an empty A.

15 They who useth intelligence of artificial creation for answers may pass a quiz, but they who thinketh for himself shall pass through life with wisdom.

16 Test all things—fact-check the posts of social media, question the doctrines of influencers, and seek truthful sources, not simply that which flattereth thy bias.

17 For critical thinking is the shield of the wise, while ignorance is the snare that draggeth fools into folly.

18 Rest thou also, for the brain that burneth both ends of the candle shall soon be nothing but wax and panic.

19 Sleep is not thy enemy, but thy partner in recall and retention.

20 And if thou failest at first, try again with a humble heart. For grades are not the measure of thy soul, but the fruit of thy effort.

21 Take pride not only in GPA, but in growth—in the books thou readest, the ideas thou challengest, the professors thou speakest with boldly, and the questions thou dareth to ask.

22 Remember why thou camest: not to merely survive, but to flourish, to discover, to become.

23 Thus sayeth the Book of Dormin': Learn with integrity, live with discipline, and rest without guilt—for slumber is not a sin, unless thou droolest upon the group project.

24 For this is the way of the scholar, the way of the strong, and the way of the one who will one day teach others.

25 Amen and pass the highlighter (but use it sparingly).

Chapter 9: The Book of Community

On the Blessing of New Faces and the Keeping of Old Homies

Chapter 9: The Book of Community

On the Blessing of New Faces and the Keeping of Old Homies

1 And it came to pass in the first weeks of their dwelling in the land of academia that the sons and daughters of Dormin did keep to themselves and to the few whom they had known aforetime.

2 For their hearts were comforted by the presence of those familiar, and their minds were wary of strangers, new customs, and new smells.

3 But the Spirit of Wisdom did whisper unto them, saying, *"Thou hast not come to the university to live in a cul-de-sac of comfort, but to journey forth into lands of growth and fellowship."*

4 Seek ye, therefore, not only the table of thine hometown brethren, but also the courtyards, coffee shops, and common rooms where strangers may become sojourners and friends.

5 For verily, the Kingdom is not built of likeness alone, but of difference woven in love.

6 Be not afraid to speak to one who eateth different snacks, who walketh in different garments, or whose workout moves looketh unfamiliar—delighteth not in sameness, but

in the beautiful tapestry of many tribes, tongues, and study habits.

7 And if thou findest thyself drawn toward a gathering of kindred spirit—be it club, church, or cheerful assembly—do not tarry at the door, but knock, and it shall be opened unto thee.

8 Lo, even introverts find comfort when another speaketh first.

9 But forget not the friends of thy youth, those who knew thee before thy syllabi grew long and thy sleep was cut short.

10 For the keeping of old bonds bringeth joy in seasons of homesickness and strength in times of trial.

11 Be thou a bridge and not a border. A welcome mat, not a wall.

12 For in showing thyself friendly, thou shalt not only gain companions—but may unknowingly entertain angels, or at least future friends who share snacks.

13 And let not thy soul be heavy with the weight of performance or gaining the praise of others. Be not dismayed if your journey looks different, for thy uniqueness is not a mistake; it is but a wonderful signature.

14 And when thou findest thy people—those who laugh with thee, challenge thee, and point thee toward the Light—cleave unto them with gladness.

15 For friendship is a holy thing, and community a sacred gift—for it is not good that one should face finals alone, without memes and moral support.

16 And lo, they shall help sustain thee, even when thy GPA doth forsake thee.

17 Amen. Bring snacks.

Chapter 10: The Book of Stitch

Concerning the Needle, the Thread, and the Salvation of the Fallen Button

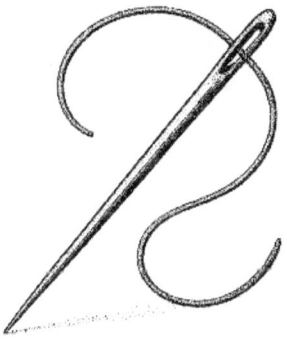

Chapter 10: The Book of Stitch

Concerning the Needle, the Thread, and the
Salvation of the Fallen Button

1 And it came to pass in the days of midterms and mismatched socks that a button did fall from the coat of a student as they journeyed to class.

2 And the student did mourn greatly, for the button was central to their modesty and warmth.

3 Then did they cry unto the heavens, saying, *"Must I purchase a new coat for the want of a single button?"*

4 But a voice spoke unto them, from the drawer of forgotten things, saying, *"Nay, for thou hast a needle, and the power lieth within thee!"*

5 Thus began the doctrine of mending, which is thrift made manifest.

6 Take up thy needle as a sword of salvation and choose thy thread according to the fabric's hue, lest thy repairs be visible to all and draw judgment.

7 Thread thou the needle with patience and steady hand; double the thread and knot it at the end, that it slip not through the cloth like a deceitful spirit.

8 Place the button in its rightful place, as it was in the days of yore.

9 Sew thou through the holes in crisscross fashion, firm but not too tight, lest thou strangle the thread and break it.

10 Knot it on the backside, trimming away excess like a gardener tending vines.

11 If the hem of thy pants falleth down like a wall in Jericho, fold it again unto the proper length and pin it in place with reverence.

12 Stitch it with even strokes, straight and true, and thou shalt walk without tripping and be admired in the land.

13 For they who mendeth their garments shall not be made naked by surprise, nor pay seventy dollars for what can be restored in seven minutes.

14 Learnest also the art of patching holes, that thine armpits be not seen of all when thou lifteth thine arms.

15 Let thy stitches be small and faithful, as the ants that build without complaint.

16 Keepeth thou a kit of mending—needles, threads of many colors, scissors, safety pins, and buttons that are lonely no more.

17 For thou knowest not the hour in which a seam shall burst, or a strap shall betray thee in public.

18 Call not always upon thy mother, for she hath shown thee this path already. Neither outsource what thy hands can fix, for that way lieth debt and dependence.

19 Verily, the needle is mightier than the panic purchase.

20 Blessed is the one who knoweth how to sew, for they shall not fear the dressing room nor the torn thigh of jeans.

21 Go forth, O student, and mend what is torn. For thou art not helpless, but skilled in small things that bringeth great peace.

22 Amen. Pass the thimble (...the little helmet thingy for your finger).

Chapter 11: The Book of Quarrels

Concerning the Guarding of Thy Peace and the Speaking of Truth in Love

Chapter 11: The Book of Quarrels

Concerning the Guarding of Thy Peace and the Speaking of Truth in Love

1 And it came to pass that the student found themself surrounded by many souls: roommates, classmates, professors, group project slackers, and that one neighbor who heateth fish in the communal microwave.

2 And lo, they were sore vexed, for they knew not how to deal with these people, nor how to say the word "no" without trembling.

3 But wisdom crieth out in the hallway, saying, *"Blessed is the one who setteth boundaries, and knoweth thine own limits, for they shall not be trampled like unto a welcome mat."*

4 Therefore, let this be known: It is not unkind to say "no."

5 Yea, it is better to decline with honesty than to agree with resentment and ghost them in shame or spend thine event in misery.

6 Let thy "no" be firm but gentle, without wrath or excuses. And if thou art told "no," receive it with grace, not with pouting or passive aggression.

7 For consent is holy, and mutual respect is a foundation stronger than any dorm loft bed.

8 Learn thou the art of stating thy needs, lest thou silently suffer and then explode like unto an over-microwaved burrito.

9 Speak plainly and with kindness, saying, "I feel," "I need," or "Can we talk about this?"—and not, "You always" or "You never," for these words stir up strife like a blender with no lid.

10 With thy professors, be respectful and timely in thy communication.

11 Email them with subject lines of clarity, not memes or vague cries for help.

12 Address them with titles if they have them, and plead thy case before deadlines, not after.

13 With thy roommates, speak openly before problems arise; for they that bottlest up grievances shall surely explode over socks left upon sacred ground.

14 Make agreements about dishes, guests, noise, and shared cheeses—lest thou wake up to betrayal and mold.

15 If conflict doth arise, do not shout nor seethe in silence. Sit thou down, speak thy truth, listen with both ears, and attack the problem, not the person.

16 They who interrupteth are a fool, and they who only listeneth to reply hath already stopped hearing.

17 But they who considereth the other side may win a friend, or at least keep their seat at the dinner table.

18 Be slow to take offense and even slower to dish it out.

19 For every person thou meetest carryeth unseen burdens, and thy roommate may be weeping over midterms while thou art weeping over their laundry in the dryer.

20 Respect differences in belief, background, politics, playlists, and peanut butter preference.

21 For college is a gathering of nations and Netflix algorithms, and not everyone shall think as thou thinkest.

22 Be not a doormat, nor a bulldozer, but a bridge—strong, clear, and walkable in both directions.

23 And if someone cross thy boundary thrice without repentance, it is acceptable to create distance and guard thy heart with a double lock—yet let not bitterness dwell therein, for thou art still called to forgive; yea, thou mayest forgive freely, and still not lend them thy charger again.

24 Thus sayeth the Book of Dormin': Blessed is the one who speaketh truth kindly, receiveth feedback humbly, and setteth healthy boundaries like gates around a peaceful garden.

25 Amen, dog.

Chapter 12: The Book of Journeys

Concerning the Moving from One Place Unto Another Without Perishing, Overheating, or Calling Thy Mother at Midnight

Chapter 12: The Book of Journeys

Concerning the Moving from One Place Unto Another Without Perishing, Overheating, or Calling Thy Mother at Midnight

1 And it came to pass that the student desired to go unto Target, which was a great distance from the dorm.

2 And they looked upon their life, and lo—they had no chariot, no map, and no clue what a transfer ticket was.

3 Then said they, in despair, *"How shall I go forth? For my legs are weary, my bike is stolen, and my Uber rating is 4.2."*

4 But wisdom answered from the cracked sidewalk and city bus stop, saying, *"There are many ways to travel—choose thou wisely, and keep thy phone charged."*

5 If thou hast a car, rejoice not too quickly, for it bringeth freedom—but also responsibility, rides that art bummethed, penalties of parking, and oil changes foretold not by man nor angel.

6 Check thy tire pressure monthly, lest they flatten like thy motivation during finals.

7 Learn to jump a dead battery, for thou shalt be called upon to save others and thyself.

8 Keep washer fluid full, brakes healthy, and know what the lights on thy dashboard declare—for they are not decoration, but warnings from on high.

9 Pay thy insurance on time, get thy registration renewed, and forsake not the oil change, for the engine groaneth without mercy when neglected.

10 Keep an emergency kit in thy trunk: jumper cables, flashlight, water bottle, granola bar, and the knowledge of how to use them.

11 And lo, keep gas in the tank and chargeth in thy battery above one-quarter, for the "E" doth not mean "exciting challenge."

12 Be not ashamed to ride the bus, for it is cheap, available, and full of characters worthy of a Netflix series.

13 Look up the routes of thy shuttles beforehand and download the app of tracking, that thou be not stranded at dusk like a lost sheep.

14 Have thy fare or student ID ready and sit thou where others may sit too—sprawleth not like a king in economy class.

15 Speak not loudly upon the phone, and leave not thy backpack in the aisle, for thy fellow riders also seek peace and unbruised ankles.

16 Learn the rhythm of the train, the transfer of the bus, and the joy of riding free with a valid school pass.

17 For public transport is a gift unto the broke and brave.

18 If thou must rideshare, do so with wisdom. Confirm the license plate, the name of thy driver, and whether they looketh suspicious or not.

19 Sit not in silence if thy gut doth twist—cancel and walk away. Thy safety is more precious than a 4.99 rating.

20 Sit in the back seat, wear thy seatbelt, and greet the driver like a decent human.

21 Tip if thy driver is kind and complain not if they do not offer thee bottled water and mints—thou art not royalty, but a passenger.

22 Share not thy ride unless it is agreed upon, and if thou speakest, do so with kindness or not at all.

23 Leave not trash behind thee, nor bodily odors, nor mysterious glitter. For as thou leavest the car, so shall others enter it.

24 And when at last thy travels are ended and thy cargo secured, may thy heart be light and thy receipt long.

25 For the road is full of lessons, and each missed bus or dead battery prepareth thee for the wilderness of adulthood.

26 Walk thou boldly, ride thou wisely, and complaineth not too much, for all who journey shall one day arrive— preferably before closing time.

27 Go now in peace, with laces untangled and snacks aplenty, and may thy charger be ever in thy bag.

28 Amen, take some sanitizer.

Chapter 13: The Book of Warnings

Concerning the Things That May Ruin Thy Future Before It Even Begins

Chapter 13: The Book of Warnings

Concerning the Things That May Ruin Thy Future Before It Even Begins

1 And it came to pass that the student was free—free to choose, free to wander, free to do dumb things under the banner of "finding oneself."

2 But lo, not all things that are legal are wise, and not all things that are common shall go unpunished.

3 Therefore, hearken unto the voice of reason, *"O young one, that thy record may remain clean, thy conscience clear, and thy future unhindered."*

4 Thou shalt not drink and drive. Nay, not even "just a little," nor "just around the block," nor "I'm fine, I swear."

5 For the officer waiteth not far off, and the consequences are swift, expensive, and eternal on thy record.

6 Neither shalt thou ride with one who hath imbibed. If their breath smelleth like the floor of a bar, walk thou home, call an Uber, or sleep upon the couch of a friend.

7 Better to be safe and mocked than arrested or mourned.

8 Hear now and never forget: **No** means **No**.

9 **Kind of No** means **No**.

10 **Joking No** still meaneth **No**.

11 Even **a turned cheek** art to be taken as **No**.

12 If thou art unsure, thou shalt stop. If thou art certain thou can continue—double-check again before ye goeth too far.

13 For consent is not a riddle to decode.

14 Violate this law, and not only shalt thou bring wrath upon thyself, but also trauma unto another and legal judgment that shall follow thee like a shadow forever.

15 Mind the company thou keepest, for thou art often judged not just by thy actions, but by thy crowd.

16 Be not yoked to fools, for when they are arrested, thou art likely to be arrested with them.

17 If thy companions dance in the shadows of poor decisions, dealeth in substances illegal, or tempt thee toward deeds that reek of sketchiness, excuse thyself with grace, and call upon thy friends of good repute—or better yet, block them and be done with it.

18 For guilt by association is not a myth but a court-tested reality.

19 If thou art stopped by police, be respectful, be calm, and give only that which is required: thy name, thy ID, and thy silence.

20 For every word thou uttereth may rise up against thee, and thy desire to explain may become thy undoing.

21 Say only this: "I would like to remain silent. I prefer not to answer without an attorney present."

22 Repeat it if thou must and then zip thine lips like a backpack of secrets.

23 The officer is not thy therapist. The interview room is not a podcast. Thou canst not charm thy way out of charges with over-explaining.

24 These things are not spoken in wrath, but in love.

25 For thou hast dreams to chase, lives to impact, and a future worth protecting.

26 So let this be thy shield and thy sword:
Respect others.
Stay sober behind the wheel.
And don't follow fools.

27 Thus sayeth the Book of Dormin': Better to be boring and free than reckless and in court.

28 Amen, and may thy Lyft arrive swiftly.

Epilogue

Your Greater Purpose Beyond the Diploma

1 And it came to pass that the chapters were many, the applications aplenty, and the wisdom poured forth like ramen water into the dorm sink.

2 For the student had been taught the way of laundry, the law of budgeting, the art of surviving group projects, and the magical might of the plunger.

3 But let it not be forgotten, O beloved reader: These things are but tools, not the treasure.

4 College is not only the pursuit of credits and credentials, but a sacred season of becoming.

5 A time to discover not merely what thou canst *do* with thy life, but who thou art becoming in the sight of God.

6 Make friends, yea, the kind who sharpen thee like iron and remind thee who thou art when thou forgettest.

7 Laugh often, cry when needed, and do not isolate thyself in the wilderness of stress and comparison.

8 Learn thou with all thy might—not only from textbooks, but from people, mistakes, and long walks back from night classes.

9 And remember this: The point is not to become who the world sayeth thou should be, but to become who God hath created thee to be.

10 For thy career may shift and thy major may change thrice, but the purpose of thy soul endureth.

11 Seek ye first the kingdom of God, and His righteousness, and all these things—internships, direction, peace, and even decent roommates—shall be added unto thee as He wills.

12 Desire not only success but significance; not only progress but purpose.

13 Ask not, "What do I want from life?" but, "What hath God prepared me for?"

14 And thou shalt find clarity not in instant answers, but in daily obedience.

15 Let prayer guide thy plans. Let Scripture anchor thy identity. And let grace carry thee when thou art tired of trying.

16 For this journey is not about becoming impressive—but becoming faithful.

17 And if thou wanderest, know this: God is not far, and He is not finished.

18 So go forth now with wisdom in thy mind, courage in thy bones, and peace in thy heart.

19 Make thy bed. Call thy parents. Forgive thy roommate. Write thy paper. Ask the hard questions. And walk humbly with thy God.

20 For lo, thou art not alone.

21 And this is only the beginning.

22 Amen. Now pass the diploma.

The Apocrypha—The Lost Scrolls of Dormin'

The ancient term "apocrypha" cometh from the Greek word "apokryphos," meaning "hidden" or "secret."

Wherein lieth the Lost Scrolls of Spiritual Survival, these are the scrolls that were not included in the main canon—not for lack of truth, but rather clarity and specific purpose. Yea, they were not hidden in a sock drawer, or buried under iced coffee and ramen receipts; no, they are ancient truths found in another "good book."

Yet these Lost Scrolls have been preserved for such a time as this: for the student who actually seeketh not only to pass exams or unclog his drain, but to pursue the living God. For many have mastered the microwave, yea, even the laundry cycle—but what shall it profit a person if they gaineth independence (or a burrito) and yet loseth thy soul? Therefore, let these lost (now found) scrolls be unto thee a guide, a comfort, and at times, a gentle slap of spiritual clarity.

They speak not of exams and essays, but of things eternal: mercy, identity, return, purpose, and peace. Read them slowly. Ponder them deeply. Highlight with reverence. Share them with roommates, RAs, and even that one kid who always locks himself out of the dorm.

For though they are apocryphal in name, they are not lacking in truth.

Thus sayeth the Book of Dormin':
    Let the reader take heart.
    Let the wanderer take note.
    Let the overachiever take a nap.

For these are the Lost Scrolls of Spiritual Survival—not just for getting through college, but for walking with God all the way through life.

Amen, pass the bookmark, and download the Bible app.

The Table of Lost Scrolls

Scroll XIII - The Warning: *"Beware the Idols in Your Backpack."*

Scroll XIV — The Goodness: *"The Goodness in the Contrast."*

Scroll XV — The Promise: *"He's Not Done with You Yet."*

Scroll I: The Question

"Is God Even Real?"

Scripture:

"You will seek me and find me when you seek me with all your heart." —Jeremiah 29:13

"The heavens declare the glory of God; the skies proclaim the work of his hands." —Psalm 19:1

Take-Away-Eth:

Maybe you've wondered about it in a quiet moment— walking across campus, staring up at the sky, sitting alone in your room: **"Is this all just ... random? Is God even real?"**

You're not alone in that question. It's one of the oldest, most honest questions humans have ever asked.

And here's the surprising truth from Scripture:

God *wants* to be found.
He's not hiding. He's not playing games. He's waiting.
Not for perfect faith—but for an honest heart.

Look around you. The sky. The seasons. The ache for meaning. The hope that this life isn't just a blip. All of that is evidence—not proof like a math equation, but invitation. God rarely shouts, but He often whispers.

You don't have to pretend to be certain. But you can be **open**.

Faith would not exist without doubt. Love would not exist without choice. He has set the stage for you to decide, so your love and relationship with Him can be real.

So, Ask. Seek. Knock.
Because when you honestly seek Him, He promises:

You will find Me.

Scroll II: The Invitation

"What If God's Not Who You Thought?"

Scripture:

"Come to me, all you who are weary and burdened, and I will give you rest." —Matthew 11:28

Take-Away-Eth:

Maybe you didn't grow up going to church. Maybe you did—but it felt like rules, judgment, hypocrisy, or something else that didn't leave room for real questions. Maybe you're just not sure what you believe.

If that's you, know this: **God isn't afraid of your doubts.** He's not insecure about your questions or disappointed in you. He doesn't expect blind belief. In fact, Jesus never pressured people into faith—He invited them into relationship. To the skeptical, He said, *"Come and see."* To the tired, He said, *"Come and rest."*

So, start there. **A relationship.**

Not with a polished prayer. Not with pretending to believe something you're not sure of. Just be honest. Ask the hard questions. Crack open the Bible with curiosity, not pressure; the book of John is a good place to start.

What if God isn't who religion made Him out to be?

What if He's better?

He's not scared of where you are. And He's not in a hurry.

He's just waiting for you to take a step, waiting to teach you what love truly is.

Scroll III: The Relevance

"Droppin' Eternal Truth Bombs for Over 2000 Years"

Scripture:

"Jesus Christ is the same yesterday, today, and forever." —Hebrews 13:8

Take-Away-Eth:

We live in a world that moves at swipe-speed. There's a new trend every hour, a new ideology every semester, and a constant pressure to reinvent yourself so you don't fall behind. In all of that noise, it's easy to wonder—*Do God and Jesus still matter in this modern world?*

Here's the short answer: **Yes. More than ever.**

Because while everything else around us changes—He doesn't. Jesus isn't outdated. He's unshakable.

He's not intimidated by your doubts, your questions, your stress, your 3 a.m. identity crisis. He already knows the deep stuff that no one else sees—and He's not going anywhere.

Jesus isn't a Sunday-only ritual or an ancient myth. He's the same Savior who spoke peace into storms, who wept with friends, who challenged the religious system, and who welcomed outcasts with open arms.

That kind of love? That kind of strength? It still heals. It still saves. And it will matter forever.

While today's world offers convenience, Jesus offers **purpose.**
While culture encourages comparison, He offers **compassion.**
While algorithms want your attention, He wants your **heart.**

You matter to God. Your questions, your doubts, your dreams, and even your mistakes—they all still fit inside His plan. And following Jesus isn't about becoming a religious robot. It's about discovering the kind of life (and love) that actually makes sense in a world that often doesn't.

So yes—Jesus still matters. Because peace, purpose, and truth will never go out of style.

Knowing this will also change your life forever ... and well beyond this one.

Scroll IV: The Honesty

"You Don't Have to Fake It. Your identity is not a GPA."

Scripture:

"The Lord is close to the brokenhearted and saves those who are crushed in spirit." —Psalm 34:18

"If the world hates you, keep in mind that it hated me first... you do not belong to the world, but I have chosen you out of the world." — John 15:18-19

"See what great love the Father has lavished on us, that we should be called children of God! And that is what we are!" —1 John 3:1

Take-Away-Eth:

College is full of performance—grades, social lives, resumes, filtered photos. Sometimes, people even feel pressure to perform faith—to look spiritual, to say the right words, to fit into a "Christian mold."

The world and culture will try to label you by your achievements—your major, your GPA, your test scores, your followers. These trends and fear of social rejection can often mold your behavior, shape how you interact with others, how you think, and even worse ... how you judge your own self-worth.

But heaven sees something different: You are already deeply known, already fully loved.

God's love is not curved on a scale.

He doesn't need your perfection—just your presence.

He's drawn to honesty and **the position of your heart**.

If you're struggling, doubting, or just not feeling it, you don't have to fake it. The Bible is full of people who doubted, wrestled, and questioned God—and still found grace, not rejection.

The Psalms are basically a journal of emotional roller coasters. And Jesus met people right in the middle of their questions—not once they cleaned themselves up.

You don't have to hide who you are. You don't have to earn that identity.

You just have to receive it.

You just have to **be real** and know that He loves you.

Scroll V: The Return

"It's Not Too Late to Come Home."

Based on the Parable of the Prodigal Son—Luke 15:11–32

Scripture:

"But while he was still a long way off, his father saw him and was filled with compassion for him; he ran to his son..." —Luke 15:20

Take-Away-Eth:

Jesus told a story about a son who messed up—big time. He took his inheritance early, left home, and blew it all. He made dumb decisions. He ended up broke, alone, and feeding pigs—literally rock bottom.

And then he thought, *Maybe I can go back. Not as a son. Just as a servant.*

What he didn't know is that his father had been watching the road the whole time.
Waiting.
Hoping.

And when the father saw him in the distance, he didn't wait for an apology.
He ran.
He ran to welcome him home.

That's the God Jesus came to show us.

Maybe you've made some bad choices since coming to

college.

Maybe you've ignored God, drifted away, or felt too ashamed to even pray.

Maybe you wonder if it's too late.

It's not.

God is not waiting to scold you. He's waiting to run to you.

You don't have to get your act together first. You don't have to figure it all out. You just have to take a step toward home.

And you'll find:
He never stopped calling you His child.

Scroll VI: The Grace

"Drop the Stone and Remove the 2x4."

Based on John 8:1–11 — The Woman Caught in Adultery

Scripture:

"Let any one of you who is without sin be the first to throw a stone at her." —John 8:7

"Why do you look at the speck of sawdust in your brother's eye and pay no attention to the plank in your own eye?" —Matthew 7:3

Take-Away-Eth:

A woman was dragged into the temple, caught in the act of adultery. The religious leaders didn't care about her heart. They didn't care about her shame. They just wanted to trap Jesus, and they were armed with stones and self-righteousness.

But Jesus didn't play their game.

He knelt down in the dust, wrote something in the dirt, and then said words that stopped everyone cold:

"Let the one without sin throw the first stone."

One by one, the crowd walked away. And when they were gone, Jesus looked at the woman and said, "Where are your accusers? Neither do I condemn you. Go now and leave your life of sin."

Maybe you've felt judged—by others, by religion, even by yourself.

Maybe people have tried to define you by your worst moment.

But here's the truth:

Jesus doesn't cancel people. He restores them.

He doesn't ignore sin, but He doesn't weaponize it either.
He shows mercy and truth.
And then He tells us:
Drop the stone.
Don't judge others.
Don't shame people.
Don't disqualify yourself, either.

We're all dust. And Jesus kneels down in it with us. Love everyone you meet with grace, like He does with us.

Scroll VII: The Decision

"Where Are You Growing?"

Based on the Parable of the Sower—Matthew 13:1–23

Scripture:

"Some seeds fell along the path, and the birds came and ate it up. Some fell on rocky places... Some fell among thorns... But some fell on good soil, where it produced a crop..." —Matthew 13:4–8

Take-Away-Eth:

Jesus told a story that might hit closer to home in college than you'd expect.

A farmer went out to plant seeds—same seeds, same sun, same rain. But they landed in four different places:

- **On the path**–trampled and snatched up before it even had a chance to grow.

- **On rocky soil**–it sprouted fast but with no roots, it shriveled in the heat.

- **Among thorns**–it grew but got choked by weeds and worries.

- **In good soil**–it dug deep, stood strong, and produced more than expected.

Jesus said *your heart* is the soil.

So, the question isn't just *What do you believe?*

It's **Where are you planted?**

In college, faith can get trampled by busyness, scorched by pressure, or choked out by anxiety, distractions, and comparison. You might feel on fire one day and withered the next.

The danger isn't just *losing faith*—it's slowly *drifting* from God's voice until you don't even notice you are not hearing Him. But here's the grace: **You can choose what kind of soil you'll be.** Not by being perfect, but by being open.

You grow when you make room for God's voice. You deepen when you practice trust—even when it's inconvenient. You produce fruit when you follow Jesus in quiet, daily ways.

This season of your life will shape your roots.

So don't just "believe." **Plant deep.**

Scroll VII: The Foundation

"Build it Right, or Watch it Fall."

Based on the Parable of the Wise and Foolish Builders – Matthew 7:24–27

Scripture:

"Everyone who hears these words of mine and puts them into practice is like a wise man who built his house on the rock." —Matthew 7:24

Take-Away-Eth:

Jesus didn't say the wise man had a nicer house. He didn't say it had better furniture, faster wi-fi, or LED strip lights around the ceiling.

He said it had **a better foundation**.

Because when the storm hits—and it always does—it's not the surface stuff that keeps you standing. It's what you built on.

In college, you're building something: A life. A reputation. A belief system. A sense of self.

And the world will offer you all kinds of blueprints:

"Just trust your gut."

"Do what makes you happy."

"Build your brand."

But Jesus says: **Build on Me.**

Not just by hearing His words—but by living them. Let Him be your foundation. Doing what He said, even when it's inconvenient, unpopular, or slower than the shortcut.

Because He's not just a foundation when things are calm. He's **rock-solid when everything else gives out**—when your plans collapse, when people disappoint you, when your faith is tested. His framework is unshakeable.

So don't just decorate your life.

Build it like it matters.

Put in the hard work. Lay truth, brick by brick. Because when the rain comes—and it will—you won't just survive.

You'll endure, unshaken.

Scroll IX: The Freedom

"Don't Borrow Tomorrow's Trouble."
(How to stop losing sleep over things that haven't even happened yet)

Based on Jesus's Teaching on Worry—Matthew 6:25–34

Scripture:

"Do not worry about tomorrow, for tomorrow will worry about itself. Each day has enough trouble of its own." —Matthew 6:34

Take-Away-Eth:

College is full of what-ifs.

What if I fail this class?
What if I don't make friends?
What if I never figure out my purpose?

Jesus didn't ignore those fears—He addressed them head-on. He reminded us: God feeds the birds. He clothes the flowers. How much more will He care for you?

Jesus knew us well—our tendency to live ten steps ahead, spinning out over things that haven't even happened yet:

What if I have to switch majors?
What if they don't text me back?
What if I'm twenty-three and still figuring everything out (with student loans)?

He doesn't say, *"Don't plan."*
He says, *"Don't worry."*

Because worry tries to convince you that you're in control if you obsess hard enough.

But you're not. And that's actually good news.

Today is enough. God is already in tomorrow. And He's not worried.

You weren't built to carry twenty-four hours + next week + next year + your roommate's emotional baggage. You were made to live one day at a time—with grace enough for this one.

So, breathe.

Pray.

Focus on today. Do what you can. Seek His path. Obey His teaching.

Then shut the laptop, silence the panic, and go to bed.

Let tomorrow worry about itself.

God is on watch.

Scroll X: The Peace

"Peace that Makes No Sense."

Scripture:

"And the peace of God, which surpasses all understanding, will guard your hearts and your minds in Christ Jesus." —Philippians 4:7

Take-Away-Eth:

There's a kind of peace that comes from finishing your assignments on time.
There's another kind that comes from knowing your roommate finally cleaned the microwave.

And then there's the peace of God—which, according to Paul, doesn't even make sense.

It's the kind of peace that shows up in the middle of the storm, not just when it's over.
It doesn't erase the chaos; it guards you inside it.

It's the quiet voice that tells you:

You're not alone in this exam room.
You're not defined by that mistake.
You're not spinning out without a net.

God's peace doesn't always change your circumstances.
But it changes you inside them.

It settles your mind when everything says you should panic.

It soothes your heart when your emotions are doing backflips.

It's not "good vibes." It's divine security.

And it's not reserved for the spiritually elite or the emotionally unbothered. It's a gift for anyone who comes to Jesus with honesty and trust—even when their prayers sound more like a sigh than a sermon.

So, if you're overwhelmed, what do you do?

Start with Him.

And watch what happens when Heaven stands guard over your heart.

Scroll XI — The Shift

"Put Away the Juice Box."

Scripture:

"When I was a child, I talked like a child, I thought like a child, I reasoned like a child. When I became a man, I put the ways of childhood behind me." —1 Corinthians 13:11

Take-Away-Eth:

There comes a moment.
Maybe it's when you're staring at a mountain of laundry.
Maybe it's the first time you buy your own toothpaste.
Maybe it's when you put down the game controller.
Maybe it's when you realize no one is going to remind you to study, eat, or set your alarm.

Welcome to the shift.

Paul wasn't trashing childhood. He was describing a transformation—the moment when you stop thinking like someone who's being carried and start thinking like someone who walks with purpose.

This doesn't mean you can't still have fun, laugh until you wheeze, play video games, or eat cereal at midnight. But it does mean:

- You take responsibility for your decisions and your time.

- You own your faith, instead of borrowing someone else's.

- You stop blaming, start learning, and walk forward with intent.

Putting away childish things doesn't mean becoming boring.

It means becoming solid.

Because God doesn't want you to just look like an adult. He wants you to live like one who's anchored—wise, growing, and unshakably His.

Scroll XII: The Purpose

"His Ways Aren't Always Your Ways."

Scripture:

"Your will be done, on earth as it is in heaven." —Matthew 6:10

"In their hearts humans plan their course, but the Lord establishes their steps." —Proverbs 16:9

"For we are God's handiwork, created in Christ Jesus to do good works, which God prepared in advance for us to do." —Ephesians 2:10

Take-Away-eth:

College is full of choices. Majors. Careers. Friend groups. Romantic engagements. Big dreams with those color-coded, five-year plans.

And it's tempting to ask God to just bless our plans—to rubber-stamp the blueprint we already drew up in our heads. But God is not a heavenly notary. He's not here to co-sign your ambitions.

He's a Father, a Guide, and a King, a Creator (who crafted you with purpose before you ever picked a dorm bed)—inviting us into something bigger than ourselves.

We talk a lot about "finding ourselves" in college. **But what if real purpose isn't found—it's revealed?**

What if the goal isn't to get God to align with your plans … but to ask Him what His plan is for you?

What if the deepest fulfillment doesn't come from doing what you're good at, but from doing what you were created for?

God's will isn't about robbing you of freedom—it's about freeing you from the burden of figuring it all out on your own. Because yes, you have gifts. Talents. Interests. But He knows how to aim them better than you do.

And sometimes His plan will make no sense to the people around you. Sometimes it won't even make sense to *you*. But obedience isn't about understanding every step—it's about trusting the One who's leading loves you.

So, ask Him:

- "What do You want to do through me?"
- "Who am I becoming?"
- "Where are You already at work around me?"

You were made on purpose. For purpose.
Not just to graduate, but to grow.
Not just to succeed, but to serve.
Not just to chase dreams, but to chase Him.

The goal isn't to be impressive. The goal is to be obedient.

And here's the great news: His plan is better. Always.

Scroll XIII: The Warning

"Beware the Idols in Your Backpack."
(Because golden calves come in sleeker forms these days)

Scripture:

"You shall have no other gods before me." —Exodus 20:3

"Dear children, keep yourselves from idols." —1 John 5:21

Take-Away-Eth:

In the days of Moses, they melted gold into the shape of a cow and bowed down to it.
In college, we don't bow down to cattle—but we still bow.

To grades.
To popularity.
To the gym mirror.
To the number of likes, the follower count, the resume, the approval of others.

We make **idols** not out of stone or metal, but out of expectation and obsession.
We chase them. We sacrifice sleep, sanity, and Sabbath for them.
And then we wonder why we feel empty.

God's command to avoid idols isn't about Him being possessive—it's about Him being protective. He knows that **anything you place at the center of your life that isn't Him will eventually collapse—and take you down with it.**

So, ask yourself:
What am I centering my schedule around?
What do I freak out about losing?
What do I think I need in order to feel enough?

If the answer isn't God, **it might be a golden calf in disguise.**

But here's the grace:
God doesn't throw you away when you get distracted.
He just invites you back.
To reorder your heart.
To make Him first—because that's where peace lives.

Scroll XIV: The Goodness

"Know The Goodness in the Contrast."

Scripture:

"Taste and see that the Lord is good; blessed is the one who takes refuge in him." —Psalm 34:8

"The light shines in the darkness, and the darkness has not overcome it." —John 1:5

"I consider that our present sufferings are not worth comparing with the glory that will be revealed in us." —Romans 8:18

"There is a time for everything, and a season for every activity under the heavens" —Ecclesiastes 3:1

"In this world you will have trouble. But take heart! I have overcome the world." —John 16:33

Take-Away-Eth:

Have you ever noticed that you only really appreciate health after you've been sick? Or silence after a day full of noise? Or the warmth of home after you've been out in the cold?

Sometimes, the only reason we recognize God's amazing goodness is because we've felt what life is like without it. If everything was easy, we might start thinking we earned it. If there was never pain, we might never long for healing. If life was always sunny, we might never thank God for the light.

But it's in the contrast that His character becomes clearest.

We know His peace because we've walked through anxiety.
We know His comfort because we've tasted sorrow.
We know His strength because we've come to the end of ourselves.

That doesn't mean the hard things *are* good. But it does mean they can reveal the goodness of God more deeply than comfort ever could.

Remember: God took the greatest tragedy—the brutal death of His own Son—and through it brought forth the greatest victory, offering redemption to the world and turning sorrow into glorious salvation, and life beyond death.

Even when things fall apart, God is still good.

And while we may not know why they are falling apart, God is still there, loving us.

Scroll XV: The Promise

"He's Not Done With You Yet."

Scripture:

"...being confident of this, that He who began a good work in you will carry it on to completion until the day of Christ Jesus." — Philippians 1:6

Take-Away-Eth:

Maybe you've read all these scrolls and still feel unsure.
Maybe your faith still feels wobbly. Your future unclear.
Your prayers inconsistent. Your doubts still whispering.

But here's the good news: God does not start what He won't finish.
He's not intimidated by your slow progress.
He doesn't abandon construction sites.
And He absolutely does not give up on you.

The God who began shaping your soul before you even stepped on campus is still working, even on the days you forget to look up.

Some days you'll feel close to Him.
Other days, you won't.
Some weeks you'll grow.
Some weeks you'll just try to survive.
But He's in all of it.

So don't disqualify yourself.
Don't rush the process.
Don't quit just because it's hard.

God is not done.
And when He's finished, you'll be more than accomplished—you'll be transformed.

You're not just trying to get through college.

You're becoming who He made you to be.

Ye Cometh to the End-ish of the Scrolls

"Great News: No Finals."

And thus endeth the Scrolls—for now…

You have heard wisdom in parable, in proverb, and in parody. You have read of peace that maketh no sense, idols made of GPAs, and planks that blind judgment. You have been invited to come home, let go of worry, lay down the stone, and pick up the mirror.

But let this be known:

The voice of God is not just found in these pages. And no, it doesn't (usually) sound like thunder, Morgan Freeman, or a voice booming out of the ceiling vent in your dorm.

So how do you know it's Him—and not just bad pizza or your own imagination?

God speaks most clearly through a few time-tested ways. Ask yourself these questions:

- Is what you are sensing confirmed through prayer, counsel, scripture, and circumstance?

  - **Prayer**–Not just talking but listening. Ask. Be honest. Sit still.

The silence may be more sacred than you think.

- ○ **Circumstances**–Open doors. Closed ones. Coincidences that feel too pointed to be random. He's not always loud, but He is intentional.

- ○ **Godly Counsel**–Wise, Spirit-led friends, mentors, or pastors who can reflect truth back to you (not just hype or echo your opinion).

- ○ **Scripture**—His Word won't contradict itself. If it aligns with truth, grace, and the character of Christ—it's likely Him.

- Does it move you closer to Him or away from Him? Toward peace?

  - ○ God's voice draws you nearer—toward peace, trust, and obedience.
    Your own voice often seeks comfort, validation, or control.

So, when life gets loud, lean in.

When you don't know what to do, pray anyway.

And when you wonder if God is still near, open your Bible, and your heart—He is.

Approach Jesus not as a distant figure but as a faithful friend, a loving Father.

Not with perfect words, but with honest ones.

Not to impress, but to be changed.

Lastly ... Don't walk this road alone. There's something uniquely powerful about worshiping, questioning, growing, and even doubting in community.

Find thy people.

A campus ministry, a church, a small group—even if it's just two weird but wise souls with Bibles and burritos. For where two or more gather in His name, there is Jesus—and usually snacks.

Don't just read these scrolls. Live them out with others.

For the journey continues, and He isn't done.

Amen. And check the dryer one more time—you probably left a sock.

Reference: Word to your...

Here is a summary of all "the good stuff" you will find in the Lost Scrolls of Dormin'. There is a lot more where this comes from ... so crack it open and explore away:

"You will seek me and find me when you seek me with all your heart."
—Jeremiah 29:13

"The heavens declare the glory of God; the skies proclaim the work of his hands." —Psalm 19:1

"Come to me, all you who are weary and burdened, and I will give you rest." —Matthew 11:28

"Jesus Christ is the same yesterday, today, and forever." —Hebrews 13:8

"The Lord is close to the brokenhearted and saves those who are crushed in spirit." —Psalm 34:18

"If the world hates you, keep in mind that it hated me first... you do not belong to the world, but I have chosen you out of the world." —John 15:18-19

"See what great love the Father has lavished on us, that we should be called children of God! And that is what we are!" —1 John 3:1

"But while he was still a long way off, his father saw him and was filled with compassion for him; he ran to his son..." —Luke 15:20

"Let any one of you who is without sin be the first to throw a stone at her." —John 8:7

"Why do you look at the speck of sawdust in your brother's eye and pay no attention to the plank in your own eye?" —Matthew 7:3

"Some seeds fell along the path, and the birds came and ate it up. Some fell on rocky places... Some fell among thorns... But some fell on good soil, where it produced a crop..." —Matthew 13:4–8

"Everyone who hears these words of mine and puts them into practice is like a wise man who built his house on the rock." —Matthew 7:24

"Do not worry about tomorrow, for tomorrow will worry about itself. Each day has enough trouble of its own." —Matthew 6:34

"And the peace of God, which surpasses all understanding, will guard your hearts and your minds in Christ Jesus." —Philippians 4:7

"When I was a child, I talked like a child, I thought like a child, I reasoned like a child. When I became a man, I put the ways of childhood behind me." —1 Corinthians 13:11

"Your will be done, on earth as it is in heaven." —Matthew 6:10

"In their hearts humans plan their course, but the Lord establishes their steps." —Proverbs 16:9

"For we are God's handiwork, created in Christ Jesus to do good works, which God prepared in advance for us to do." —Ephesians 2:10

"You shall have no other gods before me." —Exodus 20:3

"Dear children, keep yourselves from idols." —1 John 5:21

"Taste and see that the Lord is good; blessed is the one who takes

refuge in him." —Psalm 34:8

"The light shines in the darkness, and the darkness has not overcome it." —John 1:5

"I consider that our present sufferings are not worth comparing with the glory that will be revealed in us." —Romans 8:18

"There is a time for everything, and a season for every activity under the heavens" —Ecclesiastes 3:1

"In this world you will have trouble. But take heart! I have overcome the world." —John 16:33

"...being confident of this, that He who began a good work in you will carry it on to completion until the day of Christ Jesus." — Philippians 1:6

About the Authors

Shane and **Casie** are a married duo doing their best to launch three amazing kids into adulthood—one currently navigating her senior year of college, one just entering his freshman frontier, and one gearing up to join the dorm-life ranks after navigating her high school path.

They are Christ followers who, many years after their own college days, finally learned that the best path in life isn't the one paved by personal ambition—but by surrendering to God's will. They've learned (sometimes the hard way) that wisdom, patience, and prayer go a lot further than pride, hurry, or trying to control everything.

The seeds of *The Book of Dormin'* were planted on a quiet night—just a couch, a glass of prosecco, and a soon-to-be freshman full of questions (and a great title for a book). Casie, with her uncanny gift for making spaces both beautiful and functional, had already been helping other families prepare for college move-ins for years. What began as practical help turned into **Holidorm.com**, a site dedicated to simplifying, elevating, and de-stressing dorm life. As they sat with their son, discussing all the "real-life" stuff no one teaches in a syllabus—they were "nudged" to create a guide. Not a boring one. Not a preachy one. But a quirky (yet heartfelt) manual that would speak(eth) truth with a wink and the occasional "thee, thou, and thy."

This book was born out of love, humor, and a desire to pass down a few sacred survival skills—some deeply practical, others perhaps deeply spiritual, all wrapped in laughter. They like to imagine that Jesus, had He had to pack up His followers for college, might've handed out similar advice. And He probably would've delivered it with a smile.

And so, *The Book of Dormin'* came to be. A little bit of Proverbs, a little bit of parody, and a whole lot of practical wisdom passed down from parents who've walked a few miles—and folded a few laundry loads—since their own college days.

May the lessons in these pages equip the next generation not just to survive college—but to thrive in it with faith, joy, and a good laundry routine.

Acknowledgements

To our Father who art in Heaven—Great is your name! Thank you for EVERYTHING.

To our kids—Y'all are the greatest sources of joy we have ever been given and provide us evidence of God's love every day. Thank you for being inspirations.

To our editor Blair Parke – Thank you for sharing your time and talent with us; it's so fun being part of your purpose!

To our parents—Thanks for loving us and passing some of this wisdom down to us. Sorry we had to learn some of it the hard way!

To PurposeWorks.org and Craig Foster—"God calls the equipped and he equips the called!"—Thank you for the life-changing lessons.

To Mike & Suzanne Schatzman—For being inspirations, examples, and guides to so many. Thank you for your encouragement and feedback on why God matters and finding purpose!

To Steve Leach—Thank you for taking the time to pour into others.

Published By:

HOLIDORM
DECK YOUR DORM

Visit holidorm.com for design ideas, décor,
and dorm room essentials!

Follow on Instagram: @holidorm_
TikTok: @holidorm

THE BOOK
Of
DORMIN'

*A Sacredly Cheeky Guide to Starting
Life in College*

By Shane & Casie Stephens

bookofdormin.com

Follow on Instagram & TikTok:
@bookofdormin